STAR TRAIL One – by 1st 5th

A selection of Current Remote Views 2010. (Quantum 5th D) Q5 LEAP Psi paintings two years training by Military. Skilled psi paintings done first, then connected to their corresponding match, afterwards.

Canadian Military CF-18 Hornets

Q5 LEAP – Sun Fire Ops
Edmonton, Alberta, Canada

ISBN # 9780981147093
Copyright © 1st 5th May 12, 2010

I was trained by Military that is American and Canadian/Nato troops all of it. The material is not the daily work I do, it is but a small excerpt of such. I work continuously, monitored and babysat and sometimes sat on! since Feb. 2006. Q5 Leap is esoteric, Oracle in nature, very much like the I Ching, and it is an arduous process. Entirely Quantum 5th in nature, not linear but not excluding the linear component. This work is the STAR TRAIL as found by others, among them Graham Hancock and Robert Bauval, scholars with many bestsellers on the subject of the Time Tunnel phenomenon- *Message of the Sphinx*. I also use a decoding of the Remote View material of the ancient Egyptians, in particular one papyrus holistically presenting a complete encapsulation of the SpaceTimeLight Quantum 5D LEAP.

This work is accessed and linked to the current conflict, of Military significance. Some of the Law use it at times for 'tips'. Endorsed by talent such as Gov. Arnold Schwarzenegger, Tom Cruise, Kevin Costner, and Bruce Willis, and Slyvester Stallone. I work volunteer and freelance. Open Stargate and Q5 LEAP are owned and operated by myself with a team of enthusiastic helpers. Hopefully in the future, soon, there will be others involved in developing this fascinating and absolutely astounding ability to take us into the Quantum FUTURE CERTAIN of Inter-Galactic wonders and achievements. I am IN the Time Tunnel it runs both forwards and backwards. I do the best I can...it's a lifelong pursuit of understanding the Hypershift. I have other books online for free filled with color visuals and some for sale at Amazon.com

-. I am allowed to use Fox Cable News. They access my daily written Remote Viewing scripting for their own purposes - however, not concepts. Hence the reliance on US material, as well.

 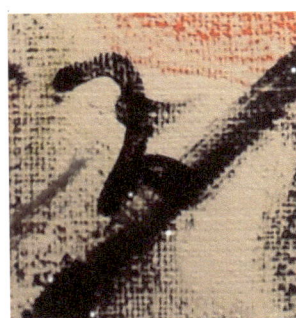

REMOTE VIEWING - Q5 LEAP psi painting by 1st 5th

Kaya Korean Bow; Canadian Air Force Jet trail Bow Remote Views (below)

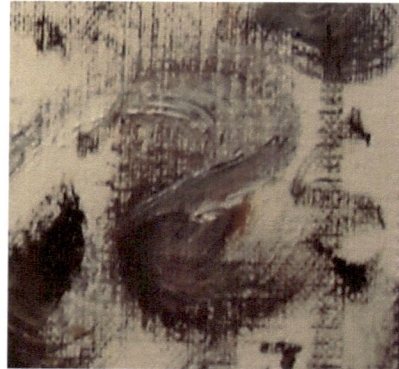
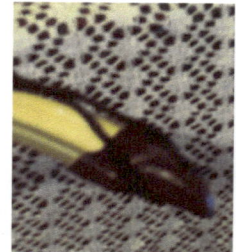

Feathering and notches of arrow; showing described visually as 'ears'

Q5 LEAP Kaya Korean Bow tips

Canadian Air Force- Jet Trails matching my Kaya Korean Bow
Kaya bow style tip ends, curves and the many other Jet trail features gloriously displayed in the following photos. (Edmonton, Alberta, Canada)

Star Trail One

Star Trail One   1st 5th   7

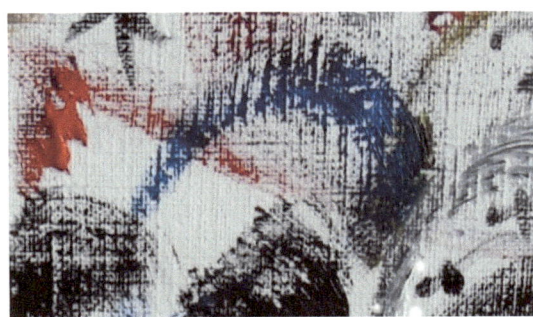

Q5 LEAP Remote Views of the May 12th, 2010 Canadian Jet's trails; crossed trails with star shaped RV (below)

The '4' is psi paint code, links to the 4 in www.nuts4mars.com for the Star Trail pages on it; next to it is a star *emote or stick man* visual for crossed jet trails; (right) double crossed Jets' trails, Remote View psi paint in white dots so you can see it easier.

Jet /plane RV joke; blades between dots, visuals descriptive of 'cutting edge'

Q5 LEAP - trained by Military, Remote Viewing - 2010

Here at Open Stargate, as First Viewer 5th D, aka 1st 5th, I don't follow along with the tv news about the weather or accidents. The odd exception applies. I did for early training I followed everything, I am more focused now. Natural disasters provide visually, just pattern Recognition. Not very useful. We have a 'help yourselves' as in self serve on those events. They are welcome to use it for their own information. I know the Canuck media do it, but they were apparently anti Western in slant led by the internationally anti War minded CNN and NASA notions in regards to this Remote Viewing. They were mostly misled, perhaps some of it unintentionally. For the large part their beliefs are not what or how this operates. That's the reason I don't watch much of the Canadian news. It's useless to me. They want to focus on things that I am not working on or with. I can't do 'everything'.

The truly valuable intelligence work done by the trained Remote Viewing, deals with Security issues. I am one person I work full time as in extreme hours, plenty of overtime I don't have the luxury to do it all or to humour or to get caught up in other peoples idea of what this is. I call it MI: 8 …it's true. I choose the Missions, for the most part and the Military and others place requests. For example- if a soldier goes missing I will try to aid in looking for them; sometimes if a helicopter goes down they will use the Remote View psi material I do daily, for visual clues; if climbers get lost on a high mountain, we search for tips. Like that, for the most part. Very challenging work, with Psi there are certainly no guarantees. That's just how it is. As well, I follow the Psi for the terrorists and truly bad guys who are out to harm our civilization. Our modern advanced Western English Christian side in conflicts. Not natural events. I helped at the odd event if the Military are presenting at them. I have intensive training. All computer pixel linked. You read some of the 'Knights of Mars' by 1st 5th, myself, from my web site (see below). The early part is not polished but it will provide somewhat of a clearer picture of what Q5 LEAP involves. Then the process develops and the most recent material online for Public reading is more advanced and again more focused.

Just I get the impression that`s what they seem to be looking for when I watch the Canuck news. Their focus is off in terms of this. I don't 'do' or follow weather or accidents. The odd rescue, but it is dependant on whatever channel I am tuned into as a regular basis. And that`s the American one for the War and the script and they chat and sign to me. It`s not like I just sit here and do this alone. I really don't.
The Military and Intelligence community are in touch pretty much continuously. Additionally, I won't and don't tolerate witch hunts. I don`t have to. I am not a witch and even if I was, it is not illegal. What I am, for many years is a trained Psi Ops Remote Viewer, or in modern terms, Quantum 5th Dimension Hypershift, or Q5 Leap; a glorified Oracle function.

As such, I am not responsible for other people`s religious or other beliefs. I don't have to be. That is freedom. This is a free society. There is nothing at all wrong or harmful with what I do. I aid …I have Psi talent and training; I type and paint Psi trained coded Remote Views. That is it. I give tips. And I do the odd linear bit of intuitive-logic that is Q5 Leap precision at times and therefore helpful for it's insight.

The rest is my developing the Star Trail and reading Star maps. For details, see the other books by 1st 5th. Learning the ropes to hyper shift. Helping Security with intelligence tips using psychic sensed means, rendered as complete color specific units via *Quantum Chromo Dynamics,* and trained Codes. In short - Q5 LEAP.

In regards to the newly released movie 'Men Who Stare At Goats' about Remote Viewing - I was trained by the Military but I am not 'in' the Military. The start of that particular movie dealing directly with this subject of Remote Viewing as done by the Military trained Viewers, I do not walk through walls and I do not stare at nor harm any living being. That aside, they did have the early CIA 'Stargate' psychic Remote Viewing program, and here as applied by the Military. Canada and America have an entente, a friendly arrangement, in this regards.

I am in contact and monitored and accessed by the Military; American, Canadian, UK and the NATO coalition countries. I work Counterterrorism since Feb. 2006. I was recruited by Pres. Bush as part of a Counterterrorism unit. I have over 4 years experience under Pres. G.W. Bush and Prime Minister Stephen Harper. Still functioning in 2010. I work as a Psychic Spy or Remote Viewer. I also occasionally assist Rescue attempts on an MI: 8 basis. I decide when and what to work on.

I was trained on my computer, intensively for over two years, computer pixel linked visual release, demanding work. This is not speculative it is a program that originated and was developed for many years in America. I came onboard as Mars Reconnaissance. This was recently stopped by the new admin. However, I continue to be a Psychic Spy, Remote Viewer. My work is still accessed daily and I am still functioning as per usual. My streaming written Remote Viewing daily material and the daily Remote Viewing Psi Painting, are the result of their extensive training and is largely a coded process, it is after all, Spyland. With highly sensitive information, and lives at stake. The Military as well do the hand signals etc as a matter of routine. The content of the work, as I stated earlier, is highly sensitive and I do not put up more than a few selected endorsements.

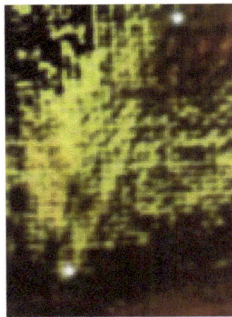 

Psychic paintings prior to seeing the item - knife cutting rope ('Sahara'); bullet

Troops Afghanistan 2010

Covering the tops was credited to me due to my *insistence* - 2006 Remote Viewer - 1ˢᵗ 5ᵗʰ

  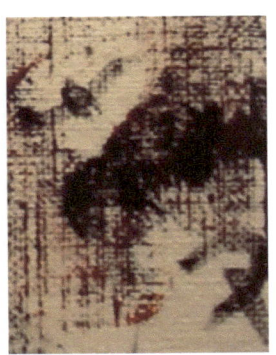

COVERED TOPS - Q5 LEAP psi paint

2010 Cover still used extensively in Iraq and in Afghanistan too, above right

US Cent Com Cmdr Gen David H. Petraeus and top Cmdr Iraq Gen Ray Odierno - responsible for Iraqis successfully winning their freedom in Iraq

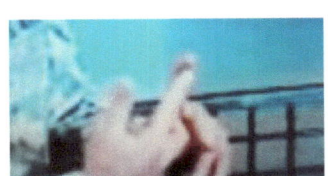

Gen David H. Petraeus -dino hand signal; cross thatching RV

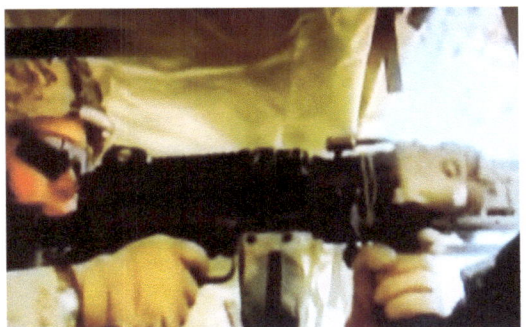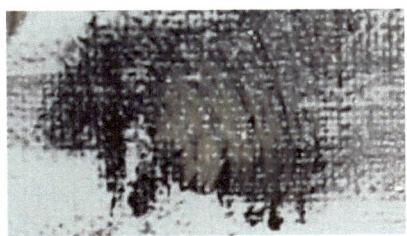

Q5 LEAP remote psi view of gloved hand fingers

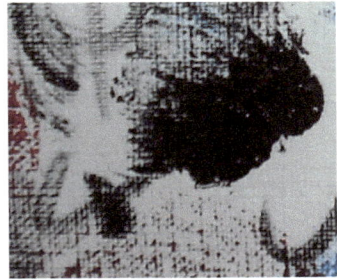

Q5 LEAP emote visual describing large guns

Hand shadow puppets; more shadow play on wall (above right)

Troops running and tunnel; matching RV emote 'running' and tunnel dark patch visual

Matching 'dot' emote figure (far left, extended photo above) descriptive of 'material'

Xtended photo and Q5 LEAP painting.

Same troops photo; while training the Psi skill the viewer paints, is shown one photo to see the matching articles. Then later a succession of similar photos but with an extended view field. It develops the Viewers ability to 'see' or sense as it were past the range shown and paint the missing visuals. Then the extended photo is shown to match up to the new Q5 Leap psychic painting. There is a coding involved. It requires intensive training for many years and is always an ongoing part of working an Open Stargate.

Window and matching psi paint (below)

One eye showing, figure in background

Second Xtended photo showing head up, dark glasses showing, captured by Psi in the Emote

One eye showing, repeat Q5 LEAP theme; match to
visual shape, bottom left of RV (above)

 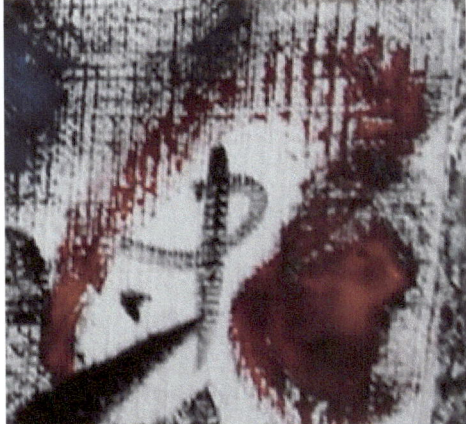

Afghanistan; matching RV of wicker and below, the crossed lines visual shape
in the extended photo (for training purposes later photos show more)

 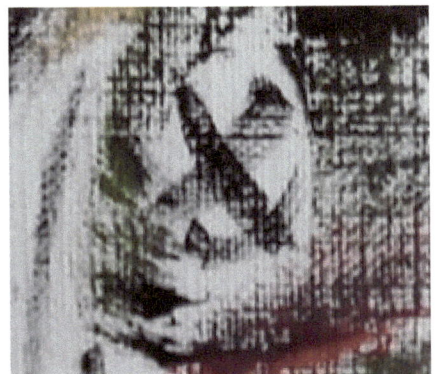

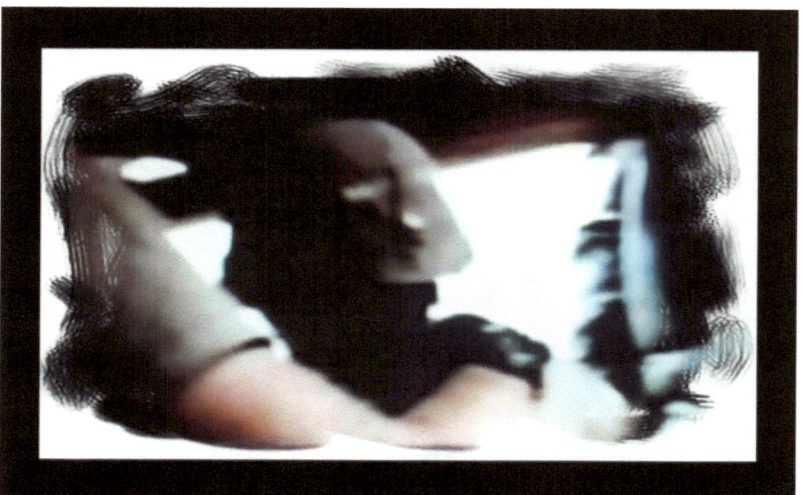

 1.
 2.

(fmr) Cent Com Gen DH Petraeus; (fmr) American/NATO Gen Stanley Mc Chrystal

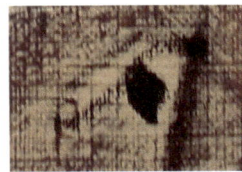 1. thumb tip
 2. Curved end

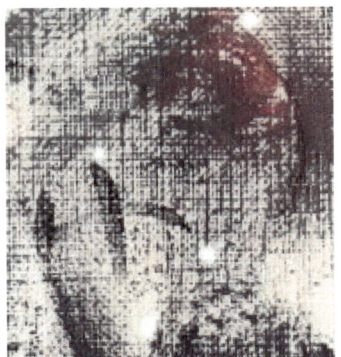  

Cdn Army General Rick Hillier, author 'A Soldier First'; Sen John McCain, RV

 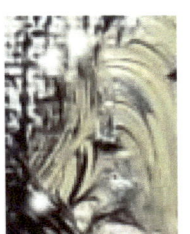 

Col. Oliver North ('War Stories') finger signals matching RV in dots, tight and curves

Desert Rats - Marines in Afghanistan June 1st, 2010; and matching Q5 LEAP

Various hoses, structure Remote View psi painting, match to photo of Marines; Bent antennae shape

Grey vehicle match; Afghanis in desert

Already 110 degrees, RV lid of the water bottle

  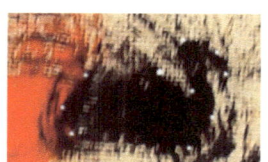

Marines, camels in desert with RV and earlier RV of a sitting camel

Iraq - Operation New Dawn

   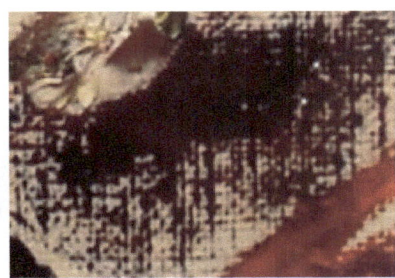

Kneeling with pack and gun, with emote visuals; vehicle with pattern shapes

 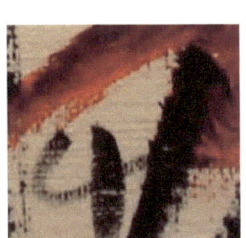  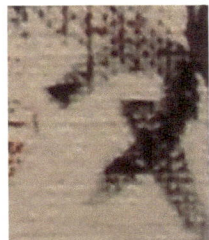

Soldier's hand hanging down and turning with matching emote RV

Gun resting on wall with psi painting RV visuals at right

Troops at market, helmet patterns with Remote View

Containment efforts of the BP Gulf of Mexico Oil spill

Adm. Thad Allen and Gulf of Mexico BP black oil spill at sea bottom;
RV match to the spill (psi- painted Apr. 30);
Thumb tip up; matching hand thumb tip RV May 14, 2010

Research vessel, mad scientists working of fixing oil spill…used a thin tube inserted into the leaking pipe, one mile down, to fix it, May 16, 2010.

I did assist with Q5 Leap, not a linear process. (above) The contraption I called very 'Mosquito Coast' starring Harrison Ford made problematic ice-slush, aptly enough. I managed a crude diagram of a thinner pipe extending down inside. As the rest of the space seemed non essential to me. They did finally settle on a narrow tube being inserted in that they sucked up the oil with to the ship above. With other science adjustments such as methanol so it didn't freeze at such great depth etc. But hey, I did assist as it was a timely enough correct assessment as to keeping it the much smaller tube version that did it. Credit when it's due, eh. Especially for the psi of it all.
Next trouble with the siphon method, was an inexplicable decrease in the amount being drawn up. The Q5 LEAP showed a possible hit by a large shark. Not all that

surprising when you think about it. The billowing oil likely attracted it or them to check it out. The likelihood of interference would be high, given this Remote View visual of a shark. There is an emote of something aquatic on the line, and a tooth.

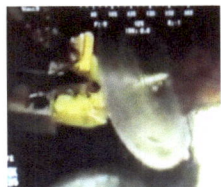  

Q5 LEAP Psi painting of Saw (left); and of garden hose RV as a visual *descriptive*

I make suggestions as I do the Q5 LEAP …we type in streaming Remote Viewing not just the trained Psi paintings. I suggested a *rubber* seal and then a *splitter*.

  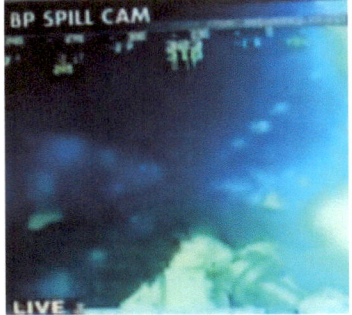

Coast Guard Admiral Thad Allen; Dino 'T-Rex' emote; live cam- Oil spill ocean floor July 11/2010- a tighter cap going on with a probable for successfully stopping the flow.

US Navy blimp also aiding in the oil spill disaster rescue and recovery efforts

 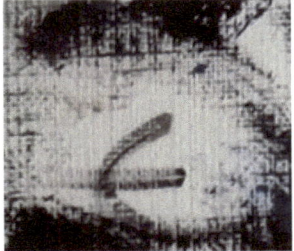

Armed Services meeting June 16, 2010 - hand signals and matching Remote Views

USA Secretary of Defense Robert Gates - hand signal to 1st 5th - bent hand

US Military Central Command Gen. David H. Petraeus- credited with Iraq surge/Win hand signals - tight fingers; Clasped hand - thumb tip and interlinking fingers RV

corner square formation- Gen Caldwell 'corner square' re: Zarqawi strike in June 2006; 06/07/2006 Maj Gen William B Caldwell IV with dead Terrorist Zarqawi, Iraq (above, right)

Q5 LEAP Remote View psi painting (above, 3rd from left) by 1st 5th of the air strike on this super bad guy Terrorist Zarqawi, Iraq; painted 06/07/2006

Getting Zarqawi was credited to General Stanley Mc Chrystal.   Q5 LEAP

General Paxton (USA); matching tight fingers - tension/cohesion to the RV;
water bottle lid next to him, matching Psi Remote View painting (top right)

Chairman Joint Chiefs of Staff Admiral Mike Mullen; tight fingers-signal; Q5 LEAP psi

 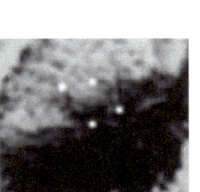 

Dutch Navy rescuing German crew from Somalian Pirates, Indian Ocean;
psi paint of helmet top (between dots to make it easier to see, viewed from top down);
emote of 'fighting pirates' (above, at far right)

Canadian Navy Post and Q5 LEAP Psi match; Seal flipper and Psi painting

Q5 LEAP - US Seals amazing simultaneous 3 shots rescuing Capt. Phillips Captured by Pirates; NATO/Canadian Warship Winnipeg fighting Pirates

April 17th 2009 US Seals rescue Captain Phillips from Somalian Pirates; Seals swimming with guns (above); matching Q5 LEAP (above right)

   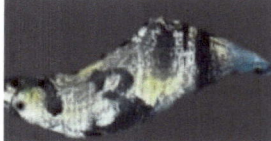

Q5 LEAP Psi painting of long shot, pre 3 simultaneous shots accomplished by Seals to rescue the Capt. Seen above with the Captain of the USS Bainbridge who gave the order to shoot; Seal hat brim and matching Remote View (above right)

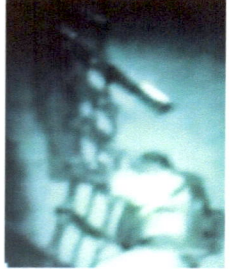   

Warship Winnipeg, Canadian on ladder match to Q5 LEAP; along with Seal flipper; Canadians took on Pirates off the Coast of Somalia

Soldiers training for last deployment to Afghan. 2010 (Quebec, Canada)

Q5 LEAP training and emotes; note the tank emote visual (right)

Cmdr. Peter Clifford, Medical Officer associated visuals in RV above

Canadian Military Helicopter; Q5 LEAP matching visuals and emote figure

SPACE X launch Falcon 9 cargo ship ...into the Future of Space Adventure!

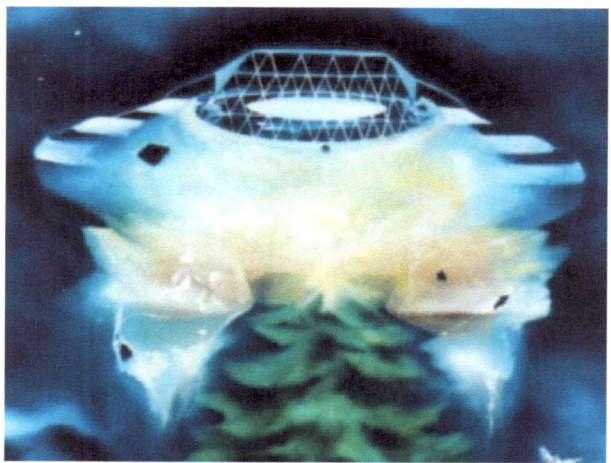

Q5 LEAP Psi painting by 1st 5th captures Falcon 9 lift off June 4, 2010

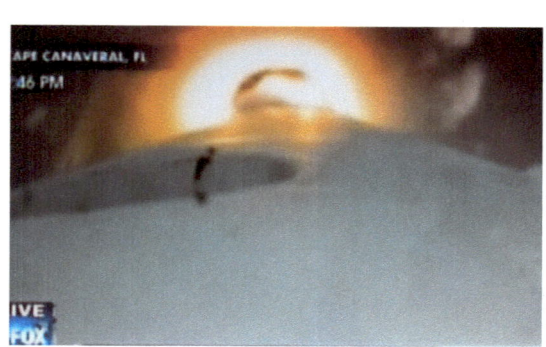
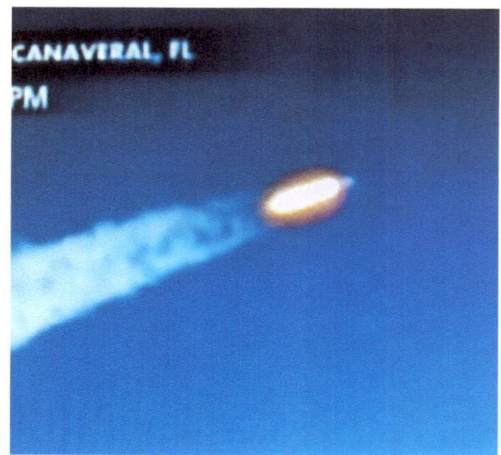

'Terminator 2: Extreme' starring California Governor Arnold Schwarzenegger

Large gun components match to photo above from 'Terminator 2: Extreme'; face with matching RV face/nose (above, right)

  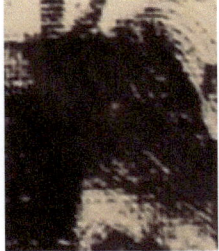 
pleated form and corresponding psi paint visual; 1st 5th dino artefact match to one in movie 'Terminator 2: Extreme'

Sgt. Daniel Biskey US Army Team

Wounded Warrior Archery and matching Q5 Leap psi paintings of Bow (below); Archer, bow, and arrow tip emotes.

Bow & tips

Bow curve

Q5 LEAP Psi Remote Viewing painting by 1st 5th to the movie- AVATAR
Each Psi painting takes under 4 minutes to complete. Psi is v>c confirmed
Race between 1st 5th and the Phoenix Lander from orbit to surface of Mars
(details pg 68 & in 'Knights of Mars' - www.nuts4mars.com)

 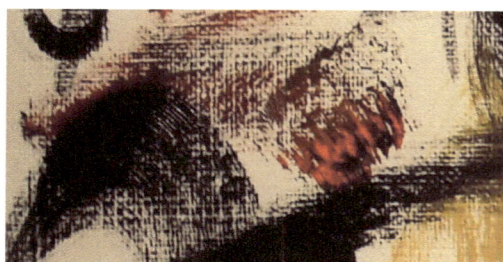

Edmonton, Alberta; Police bicycling with corresponding Q5 Leap Psi painting of bikes etc.

Edmonton, Alberta Police stop with matching Q5 Leap- red stripes and yellow/X vest

June 5th, 2010 Tekoa, Washington (US), Whitman County Sheriff's office: bad guy - chased - taunting, doughnuts, hand gestures - *stalled* - Arrested...

Canadian Navy Centennial 2010

Halifax Harbour June 29th, 2010

Communications Flag ship (retired)

HMSC Montreal - testing new replacement helicopters for Sea Kings;
Navy hats tossed into air in unison, Remote View (above, right)

Canadian Military Diver - casualty, Afghanistan, 2010

Canadian Petty Officer Second Class Craig Blake, explosives disposal expert, with Fleet Diving Unit Atlantic (Halifax); killed by an IED May 4th, 2010

HMSC Corner Brook one of four Canadian Victoria Class Submarines

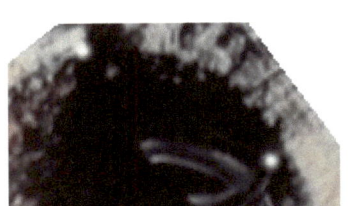 

Quantum 5th Remote Viewing psychic paintings by 1st 5th

 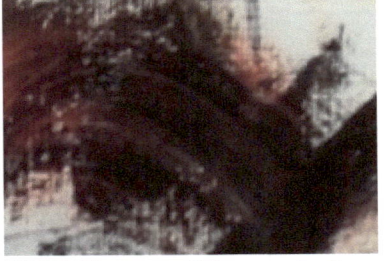

Canadian Coast Guard vessel; matching Q5 LEAP Remote View painting

US Navy show in NY City harbour May 26th, 2010

US Navy ship 'crows nest' modern style with it's Q5 LEAP Psi paint;
Old ship Crow's nest at an angle, Remote Viewing (above at far right)

Ship's Oar

Special Ops (in Afghanistan, 2010) Q5 LEAP
Psi Remote View painting of Dog helper

Dog Emote form
note the tongue's dark inner colouring
match to the bottom of the stick form
emote, a Remote View precision marker

Top Afghanistan, 2010- Spec. Ops. General Stanley Mc Chrystal

Original psi painting done with 2 separate Quantum 5th D Leaps to the same rock on Mars (NASA's MER Mar's Exploration Rover photo confirmed *after* paintings, as per the usual Remote Viewing process); see the ebook *Knights of Mars* by 1st 5th

Mars is not a water world now by any standards. Costner is obviously half fish.
I put Costner on Mars front and center in that Q5 LEAP 'Face On Mars' psi painting.
Waterworld starring Kevin Costner is timely Q5 Leap in terms of time context with the American Gulf oil spill. His amazing acuity with the development of the oil and water separation outfit, capable of 200 gallons per minute.

Remote View emote figure for Kevin Costner and his *Waterworld* dolphin oil spill rescue attempt

Q5 LEAP flashing *Pliosaur* - in Quantum 5th D SpaceTimeLight fashion, the arrow of time runs both forwards and backwards, enabling Remote Views of dinosaurs

The *Pliosaur* Remote View actually had a greenish cast to it when it was wet paint, a grey green wet glistening ….the flashing Pliosaur …it's part of Kevin Costner's emote and there is a dolphin fin worked in too. It has an extra 'wet' layer to it. I recognize them. Dolphins are on psychic lanes too. I can tell as I paint the dolphin marker. Dolphins have been known to save humans stranded out at sea. It's a descriptive worked in. for the water rescue. Costner is a water lover. The mutant in that Waterworld was himself. His descriptive is 'he is real' as Schwarz gets 'he is 'realized' and Cruise gets 'realization' and Willis…is just REAL. That's his message- *realness.* These are Q5 LEAP markers. The Physical Reality of the Quantum layering is very real and very proven they use HAL actually it is called the LHC the Large HALdron Collidor however that is spelled. Super fast atomic particle smashing…and they take pictures. And then the scientists sit and marvel and dream up words to describe what they see. And quantum time arrows go both forwards and Backwards in Quantum 5th D reality. An Earth formed Reality like the life and death that the Real Troops deal with as their reason for being.

I am *on the Star Trail*- it's descriptive and location. Many in the Military and some in Security ops, such as the Police, are on the Star Trail. Determined by traits of protection and survival as much as our creativity and advancement elements. Essential to us, as sentient beings. Q5 LEAP shows as well with some of the artists, talent like Cruise and Costner, Schwarz and Willis are on the Star Trail. We see it in their specific selections and what surfaced to and via them. You can SEE it. They're not just 'reading me, the viewer' …that would be me reading them. That's not what you see.

The movie *Avatar* is not exactly on the trail but in Viewing terms it simply IS as a View unit, creatively, by virtue of its being Science Fiction. Since Science Fiction itself is descriptive of future, and planets and deepside and …that's just it's nature. But these Viewers are focused …it's their natural psi showing. I read enough sci fi to be able to make that determination. It's factual. You can see it.

Now, the value of that particular sci fi is the timely insertion of the disabled guy being the significant player. It's timely for our culture. To get past the notion of being disabled somehow making you inferior. We are entered deeply into a digital virtual world. It's not physicality that limits us the same as it was pre digital. That's a cultural advancement. Not exactly RV, more like certain Future.

There are movies that show hi tech advancements. They are progressive in our creative culture. Not exactly RV. It's not the Psi, it's just the natural advancement of our entire science and creative Culture. Those are NOT psi indicators. Psi is a 5th leap …talent. These are just surfaced in the video as visual/audio mediums. Not medium as the psychics use the term. Just the artistic fields. It shows up, we have to make that distinction.

Waterworld starring Kevin Costner Psi SpaceTime marker-Light visuals

Star Trail One   1ˢᵗ 5ᵗʰ   43

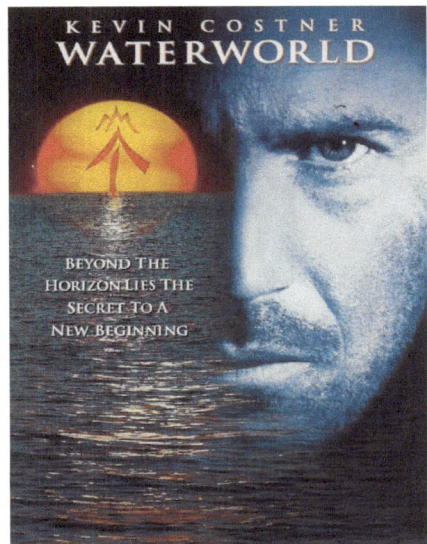

Dolphin fin

Gun scene from MI: 2; gun emote RV; (below) gun from 'Knight & Day'

 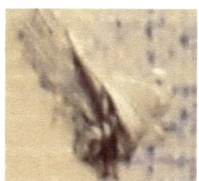 

'I Spy' starring Owen Wilson and Eddie Murphy; Stealth markers; ship RV; Stealth

'I Spy' .....'Knight and Day'

Car rolling over; emote form on bridge ready to jump

Glorious Sky Trails by the Canadian Military, Edmonton, May 14, 2010

Happy flyers and jet with trail emotes

Cdn Military CF-18 hornets; training parallels with RV below

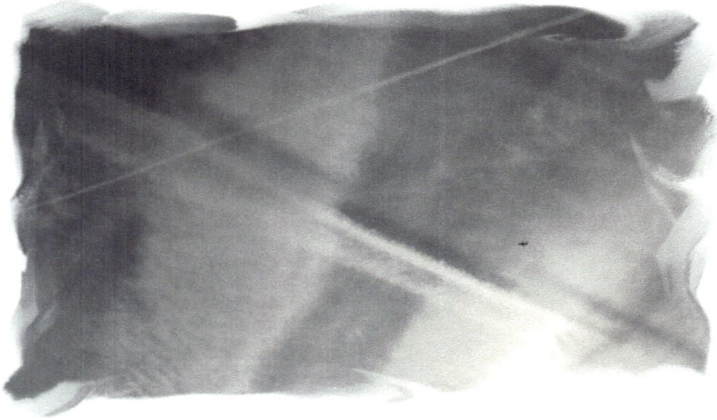

MI: 2 Mission Impossible movie starring Tom Cruise; Q5 LEAP emote visual psi-chi for a cool *MI:8*

Queen of England Royal visit to Halifax   - International Fleet Review -

Queen Elizabeth II Tierra; Navy Wilkinson sword presentation to the British Royals

Prince Phillip with Sword & Q5 LEAP RV; glimpse of Queen Elizabeth II of England

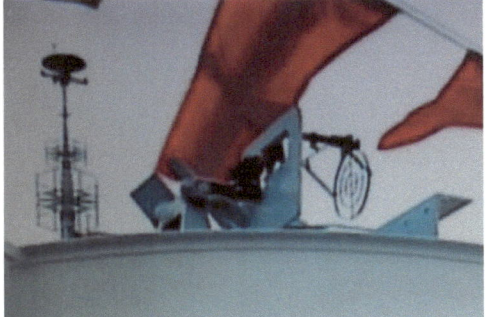

HMS Ark Royal flagship Royal Navy fleet; International Fleet Review Halifax Harbour

PM Stephen Harper, his wife & the British Royals; PM Harper RV

Star Trail notes, musings, discoveries ....light gleanings

It seems to be saying if you decode it that the other RV Viewers are surfacing. Your Gen might be another RV positive. And they are starting to show. He's all through it now, it's showing up. And the other Poetry guy, the montage artist is in this too. The ines and dots and dashes and the Times Square and other dimensions. That's just what it is saying. You would know better than me what else. The single dot, the sun symbol with more than one orbit around it, other planets would be the descriptive. I think we have OTHERS announcing their arrival. Visitation. And no they are not asking any 'nasa' permission …that's what I am now reading. Something about others and it's … now or soon or …like that. No one tells me anything, I am just trying to decode it. And RV is surfacing left and right now, as in lately. More and more. Other RV Viewers/psi links and other Others…life forms, beings whatever you want to call it. They could be Multi-dimensional leapers. Not to be lepers. LEAPers. Normal. It's a big Universe. That's good. Oh a ladder the bars in a row. There is a lot in that area. It would take me all day to read it…and then some.

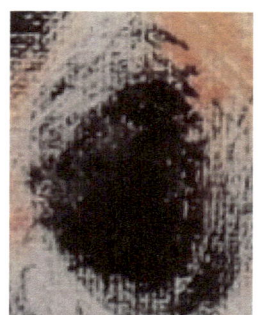 

Q5 LEAP portent- merged Port hole/AVATAR visual
(USA) Chairman Joint Chiefs of Staff Admiral Mike Mullen

Q5 LEAP catch of Israeli Air Force Jet

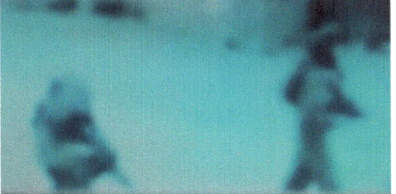

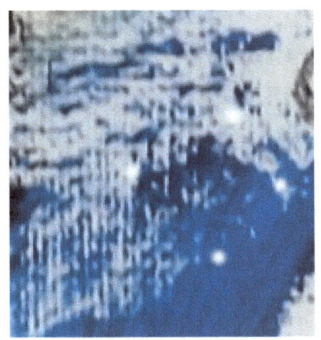

Crossed rifle butts; row horizontals, match to visual on Gen. Mc Chrystal's arm

 Slant visual

Slant showing as particularly current and relevant in terms of the protection function of both the Military and the Q5 LEAP primary focus

 US/NATO (Special Ops) Gen Stanley Mc Chrystal

'Chariot' papyrus ancient Remote Viewing encapsulated holistic Q5 LEAP
See 'Ancient Links & Future Trails' by 1st 5th for details on the timely decoding

Oracles, and orbits, the wheel of Fortune in the Tarot is Time…the arms of the clock; a clock face. And the Times Square, area and place descriptive as well as signifying a specific attack in this time context, the one at Times Square in New York City on Mayday, May 1st. The single dot for One, or 1st.

Wheel with horizontal shorts in rows; like on uniform arm and the single dot in the center, with the multiple orbits, two actually could easy be descriptive of two planets. Earth and Mars perhaps. Also, it would be Earth and Mercury.

Dots and slashes, bullets end on and long side. And guns …And specifically the General spoke today about the turning point time not being likely until the end of the year now,

and that's the end position if you read it as when it is stopped or over. The sitting wheel, the opposite of motion, as in linear forwards. Data was up, that was the Android in 'Star Trek: Next Generation' …. Yeah it could be saying before, they are defeated.
 …the hind foot of the rear dog touching the ground outside the range markers and the feet read as determinatives. (in ancient Egyptian hieroglyphs markers with other visuals were called *determinatives*. In terms of Q5 LEAP visuals are often *descriptive*.)

The 2nd race of the Triple Crown, the Preakness that follows the Kentucky Derby. I was however wrong in my selection of a winner to that particular Race. Sometimes I can indeed select the winner in an event involving horses. I went for the precision visual at the outcome position of the Race. Turned out it was a descriptive. The Lucky horse. There was a hurdle jumping Equestrian event preceding the Preakness. A large grey horse tumbled, I turned to the channel precisely in time to see it occur. The horse went over two hurdles with a roll over in between. Quite something to see. Hopefully the rider alright, he was still talking to the rescue unit afterwards. Horses can be and often are, a dangerous pursuit of happiness. It happens. The actual winner of that race May 15th, 2010 was called *Looking Lucky*.

Mer- the horse rolling was a Q5 LEAP psi catch of the day in terms of me turning The channel in time to see it happen…Such precision timing being very Merlin. Given It was a channel I seldom turn to, it was rare indeed.

Turns out that in this time context the dot was not a dot it was a square. Like I saw earlier on the General's uniform. That's precision rv and the markers are all over this guy. RV surfacing. He must have RV. …too. And I was on about a triangle and trigonometry showing in the Chariot wheel around the center. I would put money on this guy. The goggles are showing in my paint at the end place too. Just hard to see in the scan in. needs to be scanned in dry..it\s what we would have called 'he has the *feel* for it' …the feel is RV another way of expressing it.

US Marines, Afghanistan 2010

Stargate emote, multi overlapping RV themes, for the Mer timing the visuals show as A Wizard and also the RV is for a horse stepping over the hurdle; a great grey horse fell over two hurdles May 15 just before the Preakness, the 2nd race in the Triple crown.

Horse facing forwards…after rolling over and going over two hurdles.

As well as the simultaneous action of the guns being raised together, more Timing. That's what I call the Wizard's angle. The excelling use of timing. In terms of psi painting, I got the guns' barrels and the slanting motion ….ends. Another use of the concept of range, one end to the other, the leap, the a to b distance covered as range, linear descriptive of a leap. The jet trails overlapping with the gun slant.

For sure I have had psychic cats. Some are. Likely other animals too. There are other forms of psi. Like tiger woods, and his what I think was Q5 total recall and his mind working it. A to B. Like my repeat leaps to the rock on Mars, twice over. Proven. Like his. Measurable effects.
And the simultaneous psi the Military have fine tuned. Using what Franklin Loyd Wright was working as synchronicity in his figuring. Geodesic domes. There is some visual mathematical basis for that synchronicity. Chronos is time.

In my work done 1983, in Star Script there are dome like curved structures that are an echo to his (later seen) work of linking dots on a line, and considering things such as synchronicity. Multiple events occurring simultaneously. Now, that's just raw visuals, but there is also work done using their quantum visual Observations.

There are many times the Q5 Leap, being itself a Quantum process, shows up with undeniable overlapping multi links. More than one 'event' as it were, showing up in a simultaneous match. As you can see in my painting today with the converging lines that match in the same time context to the Marines gun barrels lifting together and the sky trails of the Canadian fighting jets…

Another Marker we make it…on the Inter Galactic trail…the two paintings I did at the ripe young age of 18 on the walls of the hippie building in Rochdale, Toronto, was one an Aries coming at you face on, did a few of that one, over the early years, and the other on that wall was a Sagitarrius. The center of our Galaxy is towards (the actual star group is far out in Deepside) Sagitarrius A or b I will look it up. So the chances are hot for us making it inter sol system, star to other stars, and indeed out of our solar system to the greater Galaxy. And that in itself implies Galactic exploration. Psi or otherwise. Likely otherwise. V>c implies we get ye olde teleports. Planet to planet. Likely already established. No reason to think otherwise. It's all the same Universe. Pretty much. Not necessarily exclusive. But good enough. One Galaxy is plenty! But more? Endless possibilities. Well worth exploring this Star Trail map we are now doing…not just that one papyrus, others too most likely. I would imagine there are some that are outward focusing and others more internally constructed. Holograms are not all the same for content. That's why the encapsulations.

New York City - Empire State Building; USS NY made of 9/11 material (front in dots, at right)

Display of Military precision timing - synchronicity

Q5 LEAP (US) Marines- two gun barrels lifting simultaneously

May 17th, 2010 -Not sure why, but I seem to RV the long guns on the Ships. The reversed direction of the pointing gun barrel is just the comes with of the 5th D directional flexibility. The Quantum ability is based on the Hyper shift phenomena. Often doing s a Necker cube shift in terms of direction. More like a revolving one, but good enough for you to get the idea anyway. We sort it out, or just plain old put up with it as it occurs. Looking down into a painting laid flat is another way of handling it, removing our insatiable need for 'directions' that we have developed in our ordinary usage of the linear mode of relating to the limited sensed reality frame.

Never speculate? This is an Open Stargate not some building with goats. Rather like - YOU WON'T GO PAST THIS SOLAR SYSTEM WITHOUT THE INTER-GALACTIC BLESSING AND IF AND WHEN YOU DO IT IS ALL SPECULATION ON ANY NEW TRAIL. It is the only, not the never, way you will be exploring out in Space especially Deepside. No speculation? Then stay home and don't pretend you are Adventuring into Deepside!

That's a fact. You will not be getting the goods on the Universe ahead of time…Psi and Q5 and other advances are the only way to go…out into Deepside. If other beings have developed routes already great. It won't be the entire thing ever, most likely. Unless they have other things and some of it is entirely possible, there is infinite range …but it won't be us Earthlings out there at all if you take the 'never speculate' route…you're Earthbound and this Solar System is not that shucks, interesting …
Well, it has it's moments and shit and in the future…planet Tera-forming and other things… but it's still just a few chunks of not that much…if you want to join the Rest of them you will need a much different mental approach. The 'no speculation' and one small step at a time is great…for this Solar System you won't go shit farther with that attitude.
IT'S ALL UNKNOWN X out there. Even if you do join in with some inter -Galactic core body of already done, the Exploration will not be with any 'certainty' ahead of time.
The linear is fine for tooling around here close to home planet and know.
Very well could be Psi Q5 LEAP in some advanced form leading on.

 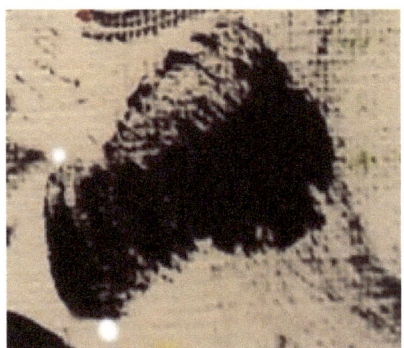

Iraq, troops and binoculars; matching Q5 LEAP psi painting

Special Ops in Afghanistan with Col. Oliver North of 'War Stories'. He saved my Sorry butt more than once doing this, there are challenges, it's a Star Trail, no one Rides for free.

  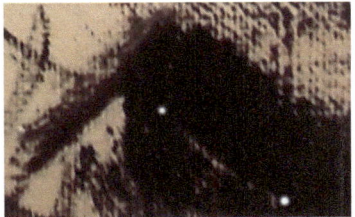

Marine hand swooping and the corresponding matching RV; Cop's hat

You could say I am *on the Star Trail*. So too are many in the Military and some in Security ops, such as the Police. Determined by virtue of focusing on protection and survival as much as our cultural traits of creativity and heart. Essential to us, as sentient beings on our always advancing path.

Q5 LEAP shows as well with some of the artists, ultra talent like Cruise and Costner, Schwarzenegger and Willis are on the Star Trail. You can see it in their specific selections and what surfaced to and via them. You can sense it. They're not just 'reading me, the viewer' …that would be me reading them. That's not what you see.

The new movie AVATAR is not exactly on the trail it IS …by Science Fiction …Science Fiction is descriptive of future, and planets and deepside and that's just it's nature. But these Viewers are focused, it's their natural psi showing. I read enough sci fi to be able to make that determination. It's factual. You can see it. Now, the value of that particular sci fi is the timely insertion of the disabled guy being the significant player. It's timely for our culture. To get past the notion of being disabled somehow making you inferior. We are entered deeply into a digital virtual world. It's not physicality that limits us the same as it was pre digital. That's a cultural advancement. Not exactly RV.

There are movies that show hi tech advancements. They are progressive in our creative culture. Not exactly RV. It's not the Psi, it's just the natural advancement of our entire science and creative culture. Those are not psi indicators. Psi is a 5th D talent. Like being able to tune into the I Ching the ancient Chinese Oracle. These are just surfaced in the video as visual/audio mediums. Not medium as the psychics use the term. Just the artistic fields. It shows up. You have to make that distinction.

Red Bull Air Race World Championships
Hudson River, Jersey City in the State of New Jersey at Liberty State Park

Some of the World's best pilots, 12 planes, 1200 lbs each
travelling up to 230 miles per hour.

Media reporter ride along

Pony Express, the forerunner of the Postal service; Mail-person emote RV

Q5 LEAP ship lines descriptive RV

Still photo from one of the Star Wars series note the matching visuals to the Modern space probe named 'Kepler' (above, right)

The large Navy ship's RV lines and the Kepler ship have the same visual patterns, so, Kepler was the guy who gave us the physics and math on things to do with Orbits …you don't go into local space without it. Just mentioning it. He was the next up from newton. Newton did earth, kepler did orbits and space lines. Not Einstein, Kepler. Newton did gravity Kepler did orbits…space gravity …earth gravity and space gravity. Einstein built on it. Got into looking at it. Kepler had his figures before Einstein came along. Just looking at the bare bones of it. Einstein did curved spacetime….Kepler did curved space, Einstein tacked time onto it. The 5th is Composed of SpaceTimeLight. Funny he didn't do it like that. But that 'oooh spooky supernatural' bunk seems to have confused things. The witch burning in physics terms. Or did you think that was that and we got it all already. Wow how preposterous when you think about it. As if. We see light here that has come from millions of years ago. Vast distances. We couldn't do that if space was 'dark' funny how them missed that. It Just seems so damned obvious. He just said something about Christian. That has about as much relevance as asking about beans or butterflies. Like Galileo trying to get the Church past 'the sun revolves around the earth' they just couldn't ….wouldn't. didn't. has absolutely nothing to do with ….I don't even know how to put that. It's just how it is. That's God's. translates as *they were wrong.* Wow. Get over it! It's theoretical physics. It's a concept. I am not looking at the figures. Let the pros do that.

It's what they're disciplined at. But you have to have the right concept to work the numbers and …it's high time they stop the witch and savages silliness.

That RV moment I pulled out of that part-whatever *Star Wars* movie, has the same coloring that's RV descriptive, to that Kepler named probe that they as in Nasa, sent out. The point is, Einstein built on Keplers' equations of curved orbits for his curved spacetime. The next step is to add- SpaceTimeLight. You build on it. What is conceptualized, learned and applied before. For the next part of the Star Trail to unfold and become realized. The name of that probe (pg 62), was Kepler.
Q5 LEAP picked up on it for a descriptive, with color precision matching. Note grey band and blue band curved shapes. With thin lines as an RV Ship's visual descriptive .
 Like the Canadian Navy Centennial, the ship line RV, where it meets the surface.
And yes, it may even take some time for this discovery to be exposed. The Code Talkers who helped the Marines were sworn to secrecy for 50 years. I am not, but Q5 LEAP sets a new paradigm and will take perhaps, some time to be grasped.
Or maybe not. This is a digitally advanced age, leaps might just occur spontaneously!

Pteranodon Ingens; Q5 LEAP match (in dots); WWII Code Talkers who assisted the Marines; said 'they would have liked me better if I was Haitian'

    Osprey & emotes

Canada Day July 1st 2010 – Edmonton Fire Dept

Edmonton Garrison Canada Day celebration
Fire trucks with matching Q5 Leap

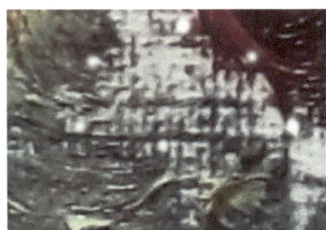

Premier of Alberta Ed Stallmach at Edmonton Garrison for a field day; helmet RV in dots

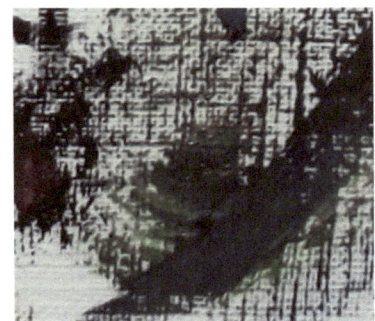

Edmonton Garrison (Edmonton, Alberta, Canada) 2010; RV of helmets, trumpet emote

Premier of Alberta, Canada, Ed Stallmach with Brig Gen M. Jorgensen; Edmonton Garrison

Q5 LEAP psi painting of field day; July 1st - Canadian Troops water bottle, RV of lid

 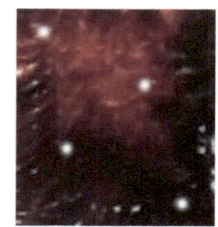 

Edmonton Garrison Military Police on Canada Day.

Edmonton Garrison troops July 1st; matching Quantum 5th Leap Remote View, note the double as well as backwards hyper shift visual (think Necker cube)

SUN FIRE OPS Q5 LEAP with Canadian Military CF-18 Hornets, Sun streak/jet emote

Canadian Military CF-18 Hornets with Q5 LEAP - SUN FIRE OPS 2010

RACE BETWEEN PHOENIX LANDER AND 1ST 5TH (PSI WON) TO SURFACE OF MARS

Phoenix Lander surface photos of Mars

Q5 LEAP by 1st 5th, psi painting done pre-Phoenix Lander arriving, painted as it was descending from the orbit to the surface of Mars. Process took under 4 minutes, for a precision Remote View. Psi v>c confirmed

 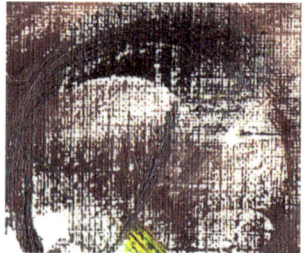

Excerpt enlarged from RV (above), matching streaks (left); chute as it was descending, (right)

DEEPSIDE - Remote Views of Space light years distant from our Solar System

 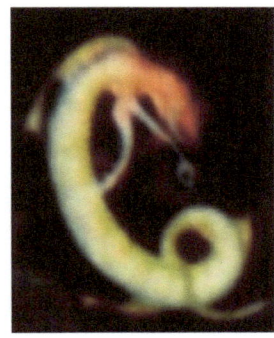 

HH 49/50 Hubble Heritage photo; Q5 LEAP watercolor 1970s; 2010 deepside emote

Chameleon - Hubble telescope photo

Q5 LEAP 'Starfire' Remote View 1983

 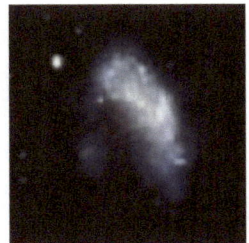 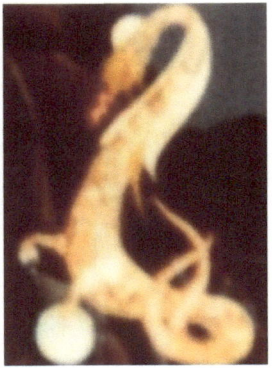

gomez's hamburger galaxy- interior of ship

Q5 LEAP Remote Viewing site - www.nuts4mars.com

Sun Fire Ops - Q5 LEAP

Subaru S106 2000 light years from Earth

Rounded corner/color Remote Viewing -Time linked to this far off beauty,
the Lord's ultimate light show, Subaru S106 nebulae at 2000 light years from Earth;
I actually had that in this time context, red dot too, and changed them to blue for outline dots.
Astounding as it may seem, the Quantum 5th D Leap does great Deepside & Dinosaur Views.
(below) matching ARC Remote View psi painting - *descriptive RV visuals*

Edmonton Garrison, (Edmonton, Alberta, Canada); RV Animal Recovery Craft

Edmonton Garrison Canada Day, July 1st, 2010
http://www.youtube.com/watch?v=hVFrhMASBXY

Notes on my trip to Edmonton Garrison July 1st, 2010 and the Q5 Leap to Deepside S106 afterwards - marker to marker:

I really enjoyed going to the Edmonton Garrison. Still in shock I got
a day off. Nice and peaceful out there. Bus went pretty smooth considering.
And I liked that nice walk to the place, no one around just empty green fields.
It was interesting. I was a bit odd but what else is new? ....at least I dragged
around a nice Canadian flag for the occasion. Made myself useful. Oh and handed
out some cards! And didn't get rounded up as a vicious psycho either.
Yeah and I got those pictures so I could do that spectacular Leap for you all.
The X in a circle in ancient Egyptian was a Place marker, location. Cities is
how they translate it sometimes, towns, places. Location the descriptive.
Gatherings. Place to place. I read the vehicle and jumped. Must be Viewers
in that region of space. Somewhere, in that direction outwards ....viewers link up.
Must be a pointer there. More than just frivolous beauty if you want to put it
that way. Functional would be one way of saying it. A Viewer is Functional.
Out in Deepside. You're not getting handed a Map ...yet anyway. I doubt there
is such a thing as a Universe map that is all filled in. it's open territory even with
star maps. Same as the nebulae are the birth place of star matter. And star matter
is the substance of our being our material universe. We are from and return to
being star matter and nebulae. Not a simple process but not all that difficult to
comprehend either. We Return. Now that's interesting. It's descriptive of our life
and death and star matter journey through SpaceTimeLight. We RETURN. It's
not so scary really. It's limitation and it's beauty all in one. Death is not a finality
same as life is not a final condition. We do ultimately Return. And it's all change.
Just how it is. The I Ching, that ancient Oracle, title translates as Book of Changes.

Security for Queen's visit to Canada, 2010

 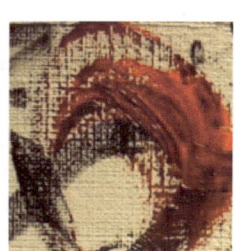 

Royal Canadian Mounted Police (RCMP); Police 'real' car chase (southern California)

'xXx' (Remote Intelligence/NSA) red car off bridge; Q5 Leap catch July 4th

'my little aliens' by 1st 5th oil/canvas 16" x 20" 1997

Amazon.com - also by 1st 5th - 'Open Stargate'
- 'Ancient Links & Future Trails' -decoding ancient Egyptian RV Papyrus
- 'MYST' (contains award winning poem *Ancient*)

Also on Remote Viewing - 'Knights of Mars' from site www.nuts4mars.com

www.ingramcontent.com/pod-product-compliance
Lightning Source LLC
Chambersburg PA
CBHW060819090426
42738CB00002B/39